***

***

Diving Into Nature

An Eco-Poetry Anthology
of Louisiana

Front cover: "Mirror." Photo (right side) by
Jackson Hill, painting (left side) by Caroline Hill.

Photo credits in the text: Joan M. Garvey — Brown Pelican, p.12; Grackle,
p. 20; White Pelicans with (Smaller) Brown, p. 46.
Jackson Hill — Spider Web, p.43; Gator, p. 57; Owl, p.73; Osprey, p.101.
Deepwater Horizon Explosion, U.S. Coast Guard (Public Domain), p.86.
Atchafalaya Basin Swamp, U.S. Corp of Engineers (Public Domain), p. 108.
Hurricane Katrina, satellite photo, 2005, NASA (Public Domain) p. 114.

**Diving Into Nature: An Eco-Poetry Anthology
        of Louisiana**

Published by Portals Press LLC
New Orleans, Louisiana USA
portalspress.com

Grateful acknowledgments: Many of the poems in this anthology originally appeared in books and other publications and are reprinted herein with permission from the poets.

"My Poem in Which Hope Exists" by Ralph Adamo, in *All the Good Hiding Places*, Black Widow Press.

"Ghost Swell" by Jack B. Bedell, in *Ghost Forest*, and "New Beach, Elmer's Island" by Jack B. Bedell, in *Against the Woods' Dark Trunks*, Mercer University Press.

"Dandelion" by Maxine Cassin, in *The Other Side of Sleep*, Portals Press, courtesy of Dan Cassin.

"River Trash" and "Trashscape Girlhood" by Nicole Cooley, in *Delta Poetry Review* and forthcoming in *Trash*, Alice James Books.

"Bayou Paddle" by Dennis Formento, in *Spirit Vessels*, Foothills Publishing.

"Two Mississippis" by John Gery, in *A Gallery of Ghosts*, Story Line Press.

"Ghost Net" by Ashley Mace Havird, in *Wild Juice*, LSU Press.

"Taking Aim" by David Havird, in *Birmingham Poetry Review*.

"What the Magnolias Say" by Ava Leavell Haymon, in *Kitchen Heat*, and "Changing Weather Patterns" by Ava Leavell Haymon, in *Eldest Daughter*, LSU Press.

"Cheniere Caminada" and "Mother" by Julia Johnson, in *Subsidence*, Groundhog Poetry Press.

"Purple Martin Suite" by Julie Kane, in *Jazz Funeral*, Red Hen Press/Story Line Press.

"Grand Isle" by Bill Lavender, in *MLR 5* and in *MyID*, Blaze Vox.

"Creole Tomatoes" and "Jaw" by Geoff Munsterman, in *Because the Stars Shine Through It*, Lavender Ink.

"Pelicans Feeding" by James Nolan, in *Nasty Water*, University of Louisiana at Lafayette Press.

"Cancer Alley" by Niyi Osundare, in *Green: sighs of our ailing planet*, Black Widow Press.

"When Pelicans Cannot Fly" by Sue Owen, in *Hurricane in a Bad Mood*, University of Louisiana at Lafayette Press.

"Ballade on the Bogue Falaya" by Alison Pelegrin, in *Sixth Finch*, and "As I Stand on a Paddle Board for the First Time in June, I Plan for October's Eclipse" by Alison Pelegrin, in *64 Parishes*.

"A small black bird" by Paul Pines, in *New Orleans Variations*, Dos Madres Press.

"Naming Leaves" by Ed Ruzicka, in *Squalls*, Kelsay Books.

"Crossing" and "Ten Fathom Ledge" by Martha Serpas, in *The Diener*, LSU Press.

"For the Hardest Days" by Clint Smith, in *Counting Descent*, Write Bloody Publishing.

"The Very Air We Breathe" and "Jean Lafitte Lane, Bayou Barataria" by Michael S. True, in *On Shaky Ground*, Portals Press.

"The River and Her Shells" by Gordon Walmsley, in *Echoes of a River: Poems of New Orleans and Beyond*, RSS Press.

"Deepwater Horizon" by Andy Young, in *Poets for Living Waters*; *All Night It Is Morning*, Dialogos Books.

"Be the Rain" by Neil Young, brief lyric, fair use copyright.

Table of Contents

Introduction

I

Robin Kemp — "Pelican Sonnet" 13
John Gery — "Common Merganser on the Mississippi" 14
Geoff Munsterman — "Creole Tomatoes" 16
Emma Pierson — "Snowy Egrets" 18
Brad Richard — "The Bird" 19
Paul Pines — "A small black bird" 21
James M. Robinson — "The Live Oaks at Colisum Square" 22
Dean Ellis — "Alluvion, April" 24
Barry Ivker — "Old Trees" 25
Jonathan E. Warren — "Full Moon" 26
Mark Folse — "Red Against Blue" 27
Biljana Obradovic — "At the End of the Year in the Subtropics" 28
Sean F. Munro — "sugar fire" 30
Mason Joiner — "Ramble and Return" 31
Dennis Formento — "Bayou Paddle" 32
Darrell Bourque — "Holly Beach" 34
H.R. 'Stoney' Stoneback — "Upwelling" 35
Randy Bates — "Golden Rain Trees" 36
Michael Czarnecki — "Autumnal Blessing" 37

II

Charles deGravelles — "Insects: Shame and Glory" 39
Malaika Favorite — "Can You Hear the Ants Screaming" 41
Kellie Considine — "Reflections on a Silky Weaver" 42
Roberta Whitman Hoff — "Dusky Seaside Sparrow" 44
Mark Marley — "Lesson" 45
James Nolan — "Pelicans Feeding" 47
Ed Ruzicka — "Naming Leaves" 48
Maxine Cassin — "Dandelion" 49
Valentine Pierce — "Petals" 50
Charlotte Mears — "The Brink" 51
Steve Beisner — "Whip-poor-will" 52
Toby Daspit — "On Bayou Teche" 54
Julia Johnson — "Mother" 56
Michael S. True — "Jean Lafitte Lane, Bayou Barataria" 58
David Havird — "Taking Aim" 60
Nicole Cooley — "River Trash" 62
Geoff Munsterman — "Jaw" 63
Ava Leavell Haymon — "What the Magnolias Say" 64
Alison Pelegrin — "Ballade on the Bogue Falaya" 66
John Warner Smith — "Compensation" 67
Darrell Bourque — "The Dialectics of Water" 68

Gina Ferrara — "Living with the River"   69
Gordon Walmsley — "The River and Her Shells"   70
Jane Goodall and Bill McKibben, quotes   72
John Gery — "Two Mississippis"   74
Julie Kane — "Purple Martin Suite"   76
Jack B. Bedell — "Ghost Swell, Henderson"   78

III
Bessie Senette — "Louisiana Pines"   80
Ava Leavell Haymon — "Changing Weather Patterns"   81
Gordon Walmsley — "Apocalypse"   82
Jordan Biggs — "What Once Was"   83
T.R. Johnson — "Double Crossed"   84
Andy Young — "Deepwater Horizon"   87
Melinda Palacio — "How to Wash a Duck"   88
Ashley Mace Havird — "Ghost Net"   89
Bill Lavender — "Grand Isle"   90
Alison Pelegrin — "As I Stand on a Paddle Board"   94
Martha Serpas — "Ten Fathom Ledge"   95
Julia Johnson — "Cheniere Caminada"   97
Sue Owen — "When Pelicans Cannot Fly"   99
Malaika Favorite — "Lament the Owl"   100
Michael S. True — "The Very Air We Breathe"   102
Nicole Cooley — "Trashscape Girlhood"   104
Niyi Osundare — "Cancer Alley"   106
Mark Folse — "Terra Bianca"   109
Martha Serpas — "Crossing"   110
Grace Bauer — "The Golden Rule of Water"   112
Peter Cooley — "Matters of Difference"   113
Clint Smith — "For the Hardest Days"   115
Ralph Adamo — "My Poem in Which Hope Exists"   116
Jack B. Bedell — "New Beach, Elmer's Island"   117

Notes on the Contributors

Introduction

Since ancient times, poets and singer/songwriters have been creating verse employing imagery from nature to celebrate, to mourn, and to memorialize the way things are or the way things ought to be. That tradition is alive and vital today as evidenced by the poems in *Diving Into Nature*. The creative expressions in this anthology mirror the diversity of experiences between us humans and the natural world in the state of Louisiana, one of the most environmentally challenged areas of the United States of America.

Not only has Louisiana been ravaged by hurricanes like Katrina and Rita (both in 2005) and several other monster storms before and since, but man-made impacts, world-wide, by the oil and gas, chemical industries and deforestation, have resulted in rising sea levels, subsidence and subsequent loss of coastal land. One recent report claims that Louisiana is losing a football field of land every 100 minutes. Another recent report states that Louisiana is ranked #2 with regard to dangerous air pollution. Texas, next door, is #1 in toxic emissions.

As the compiler of this collection of eco-poetry, I have tried to provide a platform for poets to voice their thoughts and feelings about their engagements or encounters with the land, the waters and, as one poet writes, "the very air we breathe," in this region that is home to the final stretch of the mighty Mississippi River (and its many tributaries) as it flows from the Canadian border to the Louisiana lowlands and on into the Gulf of Mexico.

Thematically, the underlying aim of this anthology is to raise awareness and to advocate for sustaining nature. And to sustain means: to keep in existence, maintain, to provide for, to keep from falling or sinking, to support the vitality of, to support life or health.

As the poet William Blake once wrote, the poet must speak to the past, the present and the future, and the poems herein do just that. Some look back and praise or mourn the natural world with its mystifying wonder, majestic beauty, and loss of flora and fauna, such as in "Holly Beach" by Darrell Bourque, "Louisiana Pines" by Bessie Senette, and "Seaside Sparrow" by Roberta Whitman Hoff. Some describe a present presence with love or a sense of loss at the sinking coastal lands, like "Snowy Egrets" by Emma Pierson and "New Beach, Elmer's Island" by Jack B. Bedell. And some poets cry out, warning of danger ahead if we do not act to sustain that which sustains us, see "When Pelicans Cannot Fly" by Sue Owen and "Cancer Alley" by Niyi Osundare. Other poems encapsulate all three time orientations at once, such as with "Ten Fathom Ledge" by Martha Serpas and "The Golden Rule of Water" by Grace Bauer.

Because of the interdependence of humans and nature, many poems certainly reflect a little more on *human nature*, though still infused with nature imagery, such as in "Trashscape Girlhood" by Nicole Cooley and "Naming Leaves" by Ed Ruzicka. Several poems tilt literal such as "The Live Oaks at Coliseum Square" by James M. Robinson, "Jaw" by Geoff Munsterman, and "Golden Rain Trees" by Randy Bates, while a few are more imaginative, like Gordon Walmsley's "The River and Her Shells," T.R. Johnson's "Double Crossed," and John Gery's "Common Merganser on the Mississippi."

Enough of my characterization of the poems. What's important is the future. My hope is that poems in this anthology will accelerate consciousness about the serious environmental situation in this part of the world. There are multiple challenges ahead: capping 4,000 orphaned oil and gas wells; dealing with the dead zone off the coast; sequestering CO_2 under marsh and farm land and Lake Maurepas; slowing sea-level rise and subsidence; reversing the deregulations of protective measures to halt toxic emissions (advanced by the current national and state administrations); and coping with the increased energy and water resource demands of the $20+ billion Meta Data Center in Richland Parish. And then, of course, there's: how to survive in future hurricanes and floods.

So, lots of challenges here in Louisiana, and it all can cause folks to suffer, not only physically but with anxiety, depression, and grief. In his recent book, *Nature and the Mind*, environmental neuroscientist Marc Berman describes how taking reflective walks in green-space parks and in natural habitats can help restore us emotionally and cognitively. Berman provides a thematic quote by Hippocrates: "Nature is the best medicine." In other words, we can be nurtured by nature. Hopefully, poems in this anthology will help us, too, for, as recent Farm Aid performer Neil Young sang, "We've got a job to do/ To save Mother Nature." If we succeed in that, we just might save ourselves.

`— John P. Travis

Diving Into Nature

An Eco-Poetry Anthology of Louisiana

Robin Kemp

Pelican Sonnet

Wide wings outspread above the bayou's mouth,
a sky-hung V of brown with kite-webbed feet,
curved grace of neck, slick crest of gold crown, neat
white mask, fish-crooking beak, stretched-flesh-fold pouch:
the pelicans are back, though nearly lost
to DDT when I was still a child,
their eggshells crumbled in their nests in "wild-
and-scenic" habitats. Grown up, I crossed
the continent before I saw my first
wild pelicans, beyond the rocky beach,
formation-flying out of humans' reach,
plotting their courses back to bayous cursed
with petrochemicals. They did not fail:
behold the blessing of each brown wing's sail.

Common Merganser
on the Mississippi

I dive but not deep enough
for that one who eludes me,
nonchalant, eyes dull, clouded
(I can tell) even in rough
waters like these this fast breeze
brings on me, tossing about it

my body as much as those —
Look! Enormous ones! Massive
as night! Still, I dive again:
Yet nothing to eat appears, save
odd bits, debris, comatose
organisms, plastic bands

that float on the surface, bread-
like but not bread I peck at,
snap on, then regurgitate,
leaving them, too, as things dead.
Where do I go now but out
to the river's center, wait

for that massive craft to pass,
leaving in its wake a whirl
of tiny things I might sift from,
as the wave's drift lifts me, as
on a glide not my own I hurl
and bobble, up this cliff born

not onto clay or sand, without
clear cause, quick as a whistle,
black out, then dive again — when
who eludes me just might peek out,
be thrown this way in thistle
and twigs, she for whom I yearn

by chance to swing to my side
or back, brown grass between us,
slick as the beaver who grabs
or he who spits from where he hides
fat pellets. I can't screen us,
her and me, from that which stabs

much worse than underbrush thorns.
He aims to kill. But I'd kill
for her so know why others
would deprive us of our groans
and ecstasies, leave me chill
out of the water, far far

from her feathers, her down I
can't stop angling toward my own
way, wishing for egg and breast,
a blessed break, to occupy
her zone despite how alone
I'll end up, like all the rest,

so dive through this murk, there work
to beak a slippery fish
to bear to her hidden nest
I must keep seeking, must lurk
near, fling toward, until the swish
of wave or wind forms a crest

and sweeps me away, flapping
madly, slapping, as I rise
a moment, the dash and splash,
poking my beak up, wrapping
my glimpse around that vague size
of her shadow, like a rash.

Geoff Munsterman

Creole Tomatoes

Ripped from the vine once its color comes
delightfully close to rosy, it's sent north to

flourish or rot—chambers never stiffening.
Fat & thin-skinned, the basin silt filters

a natural spiciness to the ripened fruit.
You'd like to think it some seed-spun

nothing, some frivolous ingredient
thickening your lettuce-ravaged salad.

You like to think it's some blood-colored
fool for your amusement fattening

your listlessly scribbled grocery list.
But one bite in, with juices dribbling

your chin you'll know even if you won't
admit it that the creole tomato suffers

its fools & spends its precious ripeness
trying to feed folks its flesh instead of

proving its bruises. Tastes like home
& home never needs dashes of salt

to be stomached. You could cut it
into quarters or core it like an apple,

sliver into slices, dice, or stew. Use it
how you want it, or don't want it.

Pretty simple as a matter of fact.
It's the Mississippi River as it drains

a continent forming more continent
for fur trappers hunger a better life

to camp out on as they hunt muskrat
snacking on basin-flavored weeds.

Trappers that'd rather capsize boats
instead of letting provincial weasels

pry what little joy a hard life gives.
Politicians rip the land from farmers

carving open oysters for the world—
what's left produces citrus sweeter

than the golden state's or Florida's
& pops its crops in spite of floods,

boll weevils, crap grass, or any evils.
Roots too deep to ever waver, it lives

through even basin drifting into Gulf
in parcels large as football fields at a rate

of one per thirty-eight minutes. Exists
tenuous at best, yet produces huge fruit

too good to not get acid-sick ingesting.
A crop that takes nothing but sunrise

serious — its survival making it delicious.

Emma Pierson

Snowy Egrets

On the Johnny Bright playing fields
one winter morning
as I passed I saw a flock of snowy egrets
White on green
white feathers on greensward
so many, standing tall on taloned feet
curved orientally
like Ming porcelain come to life
gleaning seeds from grasses
sown for public sporting fields
Oh, lovely, lovely flock of egrets
seeking grasslands
along the southern flyway
amid suburban sprawl
how long will your gratuitous beauty
grace Lake Pontchartrain?
Will my children's children
listen to your song?
will they point in wonder
at your winged elegance
against aural skies?
Will they remember you
posed in groups on the damp
leafy greenness of willow banks?
Or will they only know you
through fired kaolin glazed white?
Silent. Forever still.
Ming porcelain
standing tall on taloned feet
curved orientally.
My thoughts are a cage
I am the bird within.
This poem is my song.

The Bird

After midnight, a mockingbird that lives in a cottonwood tree beside my house begins to sing. A few tentative notes; then, with great energy, melody after melody, each more virtuosic than the last. This lasts half an hour maybe longer. After the first notes wake me, I listen, then drift back to sleep until something — a change in pitch, the strangeness of a phrase — brings me back to attentiveness. Whether it repeats its repertoire or if each song is unique and complete in itself, I can't say. All I know is that it sings. Is this normal midnight behavior for mockingbirds? When I hear it, it sounds natural and yet not natural at all, as if the streetlights have created a theater in which this singer is compelled to perform, as if it sings within a world from which it is estranged. Is that too human a judgment? It lives in a tree beside a house, a sodium lamp lights its nest. When I hear its song, I feel at home.

A small black bird

A small black bird
trapped in the eaves

flutters down
low enough to reach.

The Venerable Beade
likened the trajectory

of a life to a bird
that flies in through

one window
and out another but

what might be
the foundation of

such a house?
The mind is an idea

known only to itself
which we unreason

in the name of reason.
I fold this bird in a towel

then release it
into the magnolia night

James M. Robinson

The Live Oaks at Coliseum Square

Their resurrection-fern limbs extend
down and out like tentacles as though
grasping toward their buried brother
and sister roots. No need for metal
monkey bars, seesaws and swings.
These trees provide more and better
exercise and entertainment than any
human invention could.
They reach
like mothers' arms for children
whom they lift with easy climb
into higher branches and provide
a hovering canopy of shade
and moisture that somehow
cool the air even on sweltering days.
Shabby men and women bundled
on benches face the fountain
and its tile pool while plastic bags
and thrift store carry-ons hold
their earthly possessions and wait
with pity at their sides.
They bow
their heads and close their eyes
in either sleep, unconsciousness
or prayer as squeals and laughter
blend with the calm voice
that drones from the trees
beneath the breeze, saying
"Let the children come to me."
The voice has droned for sometime
between six and nine hundred years

in spite of storm, fire, war, and flood,
and centuries if not millennia more
if ancestor oaks be considered.
It called to the woodland hunters,
their descendants the native tribes,
the trappers, the settlers, the planters
and their slaves, the sailors, pirates
and merchants, the immigrants
desperate for better lives,
all of whom
came and played for a little while
then dispersed and disappeared
as the voice drones on
whether or not anyone cares to listen.

Alluvion, April

The river is drunk.
Drunk on time, rain,
snowmelt, spring-
swollen memories
of winter, gorged
and gluttonous,
swallowing levees
whole, burying
the batture. Even
the catfish drown.
We stroll alongside,
shrunken, solemn,
eat nervous picnics,
drink discount wine,
stay sober and
small beside
the Great Inebriate.
Someday things,
all things, will
subside.

Barry Ivker

Old Trees

Old trees are gnarled
Burled
Bored into
Scarred by lightning
And messages of former lovers
One look will tell you they have character

My bark is mottled now
My limbs creak
My trunk won't flex
It's getting so
The image of my self I see reflected
In the stream below
Is strangely alien

But when the breezes blow
I dance the dance that I have come to know
However slow

Others shake their heads
And talk of where I've been
They talk of aging
Incipient decay
I say nothing in reply
The dance is where I am
Today
Gnarled
Burled
Scarred by lightning
As it were

Developing
Character

Full Moon

Tonight is a glorious night
Alone on the beach at midnight

The moon became full of itself
Turning the sand to ivory
The ocean, a dark abyss

I stand in the presence of this organic alchemy
As a witness to the polarized oneness

I close my eyes to see this beauty
Hearing the percussion of waves
The sea is breathing

I sing through the flute
And I am the flute breathing

We breathe together and there's music
A rhythm flowing back and forth
As we minister to each other

Who knew that the ocean was such a talented drummer
An instrument hiding in itself

Maybe I shouldn't tell anyone
If word got out
The wind might be asked to join in

And who would be frightened of a thunderstorm
If it made everyone dance?

There is a symphony breathing through creation's voice
Instruments hiding in myriad forms

Red Against Blue

The small azalea, potted
on my porch, draped
in wilted clippings ripped
from neighbors nearly killed
by that frost insists
on budding, perhaps mourning
the red ribbon removed
on Twelfth Night. Bloom
I whisper and chase
these winter blues away.

At the End of the Year in the Subtropics

My son helps me to move all outside plants into the garage,
helps his father cover the plants in the ground with garbage bags
as the temperatures are going to plunge. Our papayas may die,

yet again two winters in a row. Twenty-one degrees Fahrenheit.
Worse this year than last. The papaya wilted leaves
wave their last goodbye to me. My husband finally goes to bed.

Up all night watching the water drip in the bathrooms
and kitchen, at 7 a.m. he turns on the dishwasher, lets the water run
in the front yard, so it doesn't freeze. He has removed the hose.

Despite the ice storm, closing I-10, the airport—new year celebrations
continue. Our Meyer lemon dies as well. On edge all day,
my husband hears gunfire from the kitchen, thinks he left the TV on.

New Orleans, January 2025

Sean Munro

sugar fire

on I-49 up to Shreveport
I drive the black lane
and whip the sugar smoke
with my ratty truck

when the heat breaks in October
there's a cane burn
to keep the soil rich
in Louisiana it's called
growing white money

while my wife sleeps shotgun
I dream the smoke bleeds red
with brake lights and the steering wheel
rives my jaw like a sickle on a cane stalk

straw tops and dewlap
poles of smoking crucifixes
with their arms broken off

my mouth waters when I smile
and turn off the headlights
to feel the uncontrollable darkness
lunge at me

a sugar fire does not smolder

with the lights on we're fine again
I shake a Red-Hot from its box
taste a little fake fire and the sugar
coated in history is dyed red

Mason Joiner

Ramble and Return

In the woods, I discover a walking-stick — the implement not the bug —
a perfect walking-stick — tall, obtuse, half-forked, and a still-green spring,
in late fall, impractically tall, really — I am forced to bow, meekly,
to keep from jousting with the overhang. Boots papered in the wet forest rug,
slipping now back up the deer-trail, I pause to thumb an antler-rub: raw,
salmon-hued tree-muscle, flexed and stinging, fringed with bark-bits gnawed
by friction; singing a stoic psalm, the sort unvoiced, suspired sweetly,
I puff the thin earthy air and traverse the bluff's ample gut, drawing
breath in greater measure as I go, stamping down my handsome staff
in perfect pleasure. The mockingbird's pretty-birding and leery crow's caw,
flurried folios' quiet applauding, all conduct me back porch-swingward,
plodding still and quite unhurried, to steep in the morning's coffee mug.
And at the porch, in cedar perfume, where taking off my boots I bend,
I bid hello to a walking-stick — the bug, not the implement.

Dennis Formento

Bayou Paddle

rain, water, rain –
the trip leader said he thought it would rain
thirty inches of black broth equals Bayou Lacombe
something large that I can't see whipsnaps
just under the surface
ten thousand allergens per square foot
in the form of green pollens float
in the bend where the flow slows even further down
below two miles per hour dead current
nothing moves until mid-afternoon when something
jumps for a water-strider and disappears again
under the chicory. The bottom is invisible.
Is it six or seven feet to the channel floor? The lazy curves
make you believe you are turning inward, rounding curves
invisible birds squawk, there is not a deer
nor a pig, not a third thing in sight
except 47 mosquitoes on a back trail who find me
when I step away to piss, the sky is high and gray
it will not rain but the heat is not yet unbearable.
Which way do you go when the channel bifurcates
and the cypress trees in both directions
look the same? These same trees are
slaughtered for their meat
sprayed brick red, to mulch suburban lawns.
Two tall giants without a canopy, bleached white
by death—a hole two feet wide opens
where a branch used to be
and this guy in another boat says, "Now, I'll bet
some lumberman would love to get hold of those two."
Deep inside that giant's trunk, out of sight in its hole
sits a pair of unblinking eyes, owl, peckerwood, crow
waiting for the seacoast to come swallow this all up.

Cheated by death, for a few lawn chairs, some barbeque coals
we go out every spring to pick up another couple 40-pound bags
of minced cypress groves.

Beneath the surface of Bayou Lacombe are pressed the next
ten million years' production of oil: resinous, thick,
the water resembles the mudflat below it, oil pressed
out of the hearts of frogs.
Something bumps the keel of the canoe
and moves away, sub-surface—the gray trunk
of a cypress slumps across the water, arms splayed
up and outward like a wing that has frozen in mid-air
a canoe can just barely pick its way
through its rib cage.

Darrell Bourque

Holly Beach 1952

I was ten when my parents brought me to the beach for the first time,
and it was somewhat hard to tell what of this greyish brown was sand
and what was water. There was clearly something happening in the line
where the horizon was supposed to be, some curve I knew from land

and how it met the sky. I was not completely unfamiliar with rhymes
the earth itself teaches the young who look and measure, with strands
that finally knit themselves into some kind of rope of meaning, fine
distinctions that merge into larger being. But I had never had to stand

by myself before something I could walk into like this, could climb
into, it seemed to me, as the gulf shaped itself into this bulge, a grand
stilled opacity that did not even look like water. I had surely primed
myself to bravery as parents and aunts and cousins and sisters fanned

behind me in their own play. But when the water finally surged around me,
I was ten, could never have imagined such rotary or how to hold a dizzy sea.

*Holly Beach is a long, sandy beach on the Gulf of Mexico in southwestern Louisiana. It
has been hailed as the 'Cajun Riviera' because of its cultural roots and natural habitat.
The uncrowded beach is located about 40 miles south of Lake Charles in Cameron Parish.
The area was completely destroyed by Hurricane Rita, but, as with previous hurricanes
(Audrey, Gustav, Ike, Laura), the area has been resurrected again. Recently, several LNG
plants have located in the area, but the beach remains a natural wonder.*

Upwelling

For someone who has spent so much time at the beach
It's odd how hard it is to say why, in late July,
The water turns suddenly cold in a heat wave,
And the fish die, and a rip tide swallows a child
On a perfectly calm day. It has puzzled me

For years, these indwelling secrets of the sea.
Perhaps you have noticed it, too, tried to explain
To your children. Maybe you even know about
Phytoplankton, how when the upwelling occurs
It sinks to the bottom, uses up oxygen

As it decomposes, kills the layered fish.
I walked by the shore one day and met a young man
With a rocket on his shoulder, his eyes on fire
With science. It was not a rocket he explained,
But a REMUS (remote environmental

Measuring unit), a torpedo-shaped robot
Used for offshore research, an undersea window.
Cutting-edge technology to study what used
To be mystery: Upwelling and its consequences —
The warm water pushed out to sea, the cold come up

From the ocean floor. I thought I understood at last.
It is never too late to learn how the sea turns.

Golden Rain Trees

Early November in New Orleans, their crowns
explode with copperish seed pods
and tower solitary among green
canopies that line roadways, fill parks.

For a few weeks they command notice,
evoke autumn in our semitropical place.
Other seasons, so plain it's easy to miss them,
they're like what some call trash trees.

But when their pods turn from green
to gold, from gold
to vermillion, they remind others
we're more than glad we're alive.

Michael Czarnecki

Autumnal Blessing

For you who are like our Great Maple,
Roots deep in the breast of our Mother,
Branches stretched up to the heavens,
May the winds be not too strong,
       ice not too thick,
       cold not too deep,
So that your gift,
       sweet water at the turn of the year,
May continue for cycles to come.

Those who are like saplings among you,
You who have found your place but a little while,
May the winds be not too mild,
       cold deep enough to strengthen your boughs,
       toughen your skin,
Season you to the changes of seasons,
Harden you to the cold of years to come.
May you find nourishment, strength,
May your roots grow strong and
       your sap flow sweet
When it is your turn to give.

Those of you like seeds
       blown about here and there,
No roots, branches
       just promise of what is to be,
May the wind set you down
       in a warm fold of the Mother,
Soil nurture you, waters bathe you
       till your new form emerges,
Extending downward, roots taking hold
       and life growing upward,
Slowly bearing forth the promise
       now held inside.

II

Insects: Shame and Glory

for William

1

I dropped the millipede into the bed
of red ants. No one had to tell me
it was wrong — my conscience slowly stirred
like a stick in a can of old paint.
But I thrilled too, transfixed, sleepy-eyed,
writhing with it as it kicked spasms
in tangled sheets of pain. In my uniform
— Superman underwear, cowboy boots and hat —
I squatted over suffering I had myself created
with malice of forethought and a certain
absence that allowed the slightest twinge
of hunger to lift me, thoughtlessly scratching
behind knee where a flea had bit, to get
a peanut butter sandwich in the kitchen.

2

Years later, in its likeness,
I made a place for us to meet,
a pencil drawing of a dragonfly
in lines and shadings limited
by my skill and patience, a haven
nonetheless, handmade on white pad,
apart from the profusion of differences
among people, plants, and beasts,
to share, as we all did, October.
Boy and mosquito hawk meeting
in this making: my kind, it said,
flies, hovers, glimmers, hunts;
my kind, I said, my kind, billions of us
at this moment, sucking air into lungs
and declaring I this, I that, I, I, I ... as
each of us tries to extricate ourselves
from the web of everything else: my kind
invents much isolation, art and misery.
I also drew the hand that drew
the dragonfly, a kind of signature,
a sign of damage and compassion mingled,
done and to be done.

3

Our legs dangled off the slight arch
of a small bridge into a later autumn.
With sticks and rocks, we broke
the fragile weave of light on water
shattering and mending itself,
tirelessly forgiving. We'd been hunting,
my son William and I, insects,
matching the critters found squirming
under rock, burrowing grass, air, water,
with the pictures in the book, listing
their names by phyla, genus, species,
beginning to build with these tiny pieces
the design we've been taught to call
creation. Suddenly I wanted to confess
a shameful past, to unlock and lead
this child down its dank, shadowed halls
where hurts, received and inflicted,
are mounted in their little cases,
labelled, horribly, mostly with the names
of family and friends. Why would I betray
myself to my own child? Because he shares
what I am and am becoming, and if he did
or didn't understand, he would forgive me
anyway, lead me through and out
the other side into this very day.
So naturally, I whistled and dropped
another stick, like a forgotten anger,
to slide down rapids and away.
Above the water, a swarm of gnats
roiled in sunlight like a glimmering coin;
the intricate logic of such a love
was enough and more for the moment.

Can You Hear The Ants Screaming

The battle rage where chickens dream
The hens want the right to climb
Who can hear the ants screaming?

Lord Rooster on his cell phone tweeting
I am the master of time
Battles rage where chickens dream

The assembly of fowls clucking
Minor roosters draw the line
Can you hear the ants screaming?

The press announced: The sky is falling
Lord Rooster tweets, Fake News, False light
The battle rage where chickens dream

The wall goes up, the wall comes down
Illegal aliens' cross underground, testing the line
Can you hear the ants screaming?

Doves, chickens, cows, pay a dime
To hear Lord Rooster recite his morning tweet
The battle rage where chickens dream

Can you hear the ants screaming?

Reflections on a Silky Weaver

A spider dangles on an invisible thread
tethered to the branches of the old live oak tree
branching out over my rusty steel shed.
It's lifeline slowly sways in the afternoon sun
as clouds roll in so low I can almost touch them.
Leaves stir, deft legs emerge, and the spider ascends.
Surely, hanging with a purpose, I think,
for spiders are older than humans,
their cleverness extoled in myths and legends.
They emerge tiny yet complete
with intuitive knowledge, intention, purpose
magically encoded from generation to generation.
And so I imagine the spider remembers,
weaving the past into silken displays,
tapestries rendering ancient memories,
of fresh water bald cypress swamps now gone.
I wonder if the spider worries, as I do
that our world seems to be hanging by a thread.
Perhaps spiders are eternal,
waiting, watching, weaving,
witness to that which yet remains,
foretelling of that which is to come.
Weaver, writer in silk:
be patient, steadfast, remembering
Nature will have the final say.

Dusky Seaside Sparrow*

Bird song clear
as sunlight, heard only by the water
and mosquitoes in a rush of notes
suspended over
this marsh, the little winged life,
a choral passion
on little stick legs with a surge
of breast and feather
in the high reedy grass
thriving in marshy water
fertile for
insects and amoebas
so close
to the beginning
long before humans
ever existed
before green currency
and limousines
and now the seaside sparrow
song
gone
to mute extinction.

*Declared Extinct in 1990 from chemical spraying.

Lesson

As a kid I got a BB gun.
Shot out the street light
With shot number one.
Then aimed at everything
That made its way on wings.
Until one gray day
I stalked a sparrow on a wire.
Perhaps because its eyes were set wide
Or because it was unwise
Regarding beastly boys
It seems I was not seen
And shot it in the fluffy chest
Where there appeared
A drop of blood quite red
As it hung there by tiny talons dead
That I might never kill again.

James Nolan

Pelicans Feeding

for my teachers

On land they are as ridiculous
as a poet defending his profession
to the IRS, or a busted umbrella
ambulant on two plastic spatulas.

In midair their pterodactyl wingspan
looms sacramental, necks as delicately
curved in flight as an African carving.
They skim above breakers, cresting

and falling with the sea's cadence
then rising, they plunge in nonchalant
circles, flipping into a perpendicular
dive. With honed eye intent they pluck

the living poem from just beneath
the same surface you and I were scanning
in bored disquiet, then nip and gargle
the thrashing word, bobbing up and down.

And from my teachers I've learned as much
as by watching the pelicans feed at dusk.

Naming Leaves

Six days after the great ice storm
so chilling that it knocked fear of Covid
straight out of our brains
I hold baby Henry in my arms.

We are in my daughter's backyard
and already engulfed in a soft
spring turn of sky. An owl
calls from inside a magnolia.

Baby Henry looks at a bush
its leaves shriveled by recent ice.
He raises an arm, points a finger.
Says "Phooof." Shifts the finger
two inches, says "Vvuuu."

Now Henry turns his attention
to the wings of a fern.
He can't yet fully extend
that index finger. It curls
in the direction of a frond.

Eyes luminous as twin moons
Henry focuses on a single leaf, says
"Tthaaa." Again, even softer, "Whough."

In the aftermath of the storm's destruction
Baby Henry has purposed himself
to naming, one by one, the leaves
and then, I guess, each grass blade
every stitch of rain that falls
downward through his gaze

So that I might come to know them
as he does and to understand
how to turn any afternoon
into a slow benediction.

Dandelion

Each year it takes longer to be sure
that the mane of this flower-weed is carried
     upward
on the wind's current toward the place
where wishes may be granted.

A child, age two, is not quite sure
what to make of this strange ritual
that interrupts our walk. He takes the bare
     stalk
in his small hand and asks for another

on which to blow, as I have done,
the crown of this thistle dissolved by my wish
which was more for him — not so much my own —
that he may stand on this earth, full-grown,

and remember how the sun made his shadow lengthen
into manhood — a time in which he, too, shall
     resurrect
odd customs with his own spirit's breath
among wildflowers that separate the stones.

Petals

She gathered the dried petals of her past:
the passion-purple orchid
of a love that still hungers within;
the blood-red rose of the pain that still lingers;
the milk white carnation of youthful southern summers;
the sky-blue tulip of dreams she still chased.
She pressed them one by one to her mouth, her heart
before she wrapped them
in the cedar-scented silk of a faded sachet
and tucked them into her hope chest.

The Brink

Even the trees agree with me.
They'll be cut down to make room
For more real estate soon.
Dirt dug and rolled into neat measured lots
To house energy efficient homes.
Irony runs amuck in new yards
All across this land we call the US of A.
For me too, the trees agree.
I'm in line to be cut down
Hauled away by limb and trunk.
My remaining stump
Ground out or poisoned to rot
And the obvious gaping hole covered
By a meager track hoe
That pushes and huffs.
I've seen better times, when birds
Have kept their nesting ground for years
Some high above in trees.
But now, with bigger plans laid by So-and-So,
One can hear the monster machines coming for miles,
Macho drone of willy-nilly destruction afoot.
The computer-driven tractors maul the ground
And leave their newest-model wake.
Nothing awfully new approaches. Not really.
Our lives remain temporary, the population grows.
The bees' population drops in alarming numbers and
Whatever's left of a farmer's yield exported.
So here I sit in the 21st century,
A glass of California wine in hand.
It's so damn hard to live a grounded, fruitful life.
What a shame. A crying shame.

Steve Beisner

Whip-poor-will

I'm three and it's dusk in the north Louisiana pines.
The front porch, as wide as the house,
is screened against the mosquitoes,
but lets in the air and the night sounds.
At day's end the grownups
in rocking chairs or porch swings,
sway back and forth in the still air.
My mother settles me on top of two blankets
folded into a cushion over the rough pine floor
under a quilt my grandmother pulled down from her shelf.
It's summer at the house where she and my grandfather live
alone on a hill, a small farm with the forest behind
and fields sloping down to the road.

As the dusk thickens, a bird sings.
My grandfather, sitting in his rocker nearby,
speaks softly, tells me
it's the song of the whip-poor-will
marking the end of the day.
He says and sings, "whip-poor-will,"
over and over like the bird
making his voice and the bird's name
sound like the whip-poor-will's song.

I'm four the summer he teaches me to fish
or at least to sit at his side
as he catches brim in the creek
under the cool trees across the road from his house.
Fried with the heads off, scaled and cleaned,
served for the noon meal
on the same screened porch.
Everyone sits at the long table.
"Don't you eat the fins and tails?"
my grandfather asks.
"Best part. Crispy."
Only my grandmother knows if he's joking.

I'm five when the summer arrives again.
Grandfather dies alone in the woods hunting meat.
The men, searching since before mid-day
find him late and carry him from the pines
just before sunset.
I sit in his rocker on the front porch,
my feet dangling, as my mother tells me
he has gone away.
The woods are quiet,
but in a few more minutes
I hear my grandfather's voice
and the whip-poor-will singing
his song to the night.

On Bayou Teche

the water is thick
enough to walk on.

there are ghosts
here, beneath the
surface — they come
up for air
drag living secrets
back under.

sun sinks
into the muddy
bayou, drowns.

this bayou
snakes past houses
i grew up in.
no one is ever home
when i drive by.

i stare into the burnt
coffee streaming by,
see the surface break
with turtles and frogs
occasionally. i could
stare forever and never
see what's really
underneath.

cars and trucks hum
over the old bridge. a
thoughtless plastic
grocery bag snags on
the bank. i haven't
been swimming in
years.

oak, pine, cypress
and many other trees
line this bayou, some
bending over into their
own shadows.
there are birds, i can
hear them. but i don't
see any.

my dad went
fishing yesterday.

antique shops
huddle in the center of
town. i duck into a
few, hear ghosts
whispering in unfamiliar
tongues.

who winds these clocks
after dark?

a victrola scratches.

no one is sitting
at the bar. except for
the ghosts of ex-lovers.
they keep checking their
watches.

Mother

At breakfast you tell me about
a coyote pack in the city,
the park the last place one was spotted,
just past the bend in the river,
its tail fuller than a dog's,
its ears large and shaped different
than a dog's.
Over the telephone this evening
you tell me details on the wedding
of the prince, there
will be protestors, the tornado
in Iowa took a town,
there's a plan to clone
and mass-produce colossal redwoods,
the tallest living things on Earth.

Jean Lafitte Lane, Bayou Barataria

Majestic blue heron,
Greek God on piling pedestal,
Great white egret on rock at jetty's end,
Both with the patience of Job,
And I,
At apex of angle
Stand staring at my bobber,
At the edge of the bayou,
At the edge of an inlet,
On the cusp of the Gulf,
With Caribbean Seas to the horizon,
Toying with bait and fishing intentions.

Jean Lafitte's pirates
Once plied these waters.
The remnants,
A spyglass sparkle
On sky-mirrored waves of pink and blue,
Ripples continuing
Up and into a choppy shroud of clouds.

It is sunset
And we have snuck in without permission,
As any good pirates would do.

Cautiously,
I watch as the bright red ball is
Carefully tucked away for the night.
Venus, obviously excited,
Proceeds her celestial cousins
To the twilight celebration.
Reluctance nudges me to take
One last look around.
Time and light are running out.

We had already spooked
The adolescent alligator,
Cat-napping on a water-logged plank
Or at least he was, until we came along,
Unwelcomed tourists on a walkabout,
Come to fish in the shadow
Of his marina ghost town.

Most of the slips choked with water hyacinth,
Tin roofs ripped completely off.
Scuttled boats and knotted fishing nets,
Victims of time and too many hurricanes,
This, an elderly local comes to relate,
Curious as to our business,
More wanting to talk than anything.

She speaks of acres submerging,
Reinvented shorelines,
The ever-rising tide
Leaving Spanish moss
Pretending leaves on
Saline-choked cypress trees.

I think,
Although they still stand proud,
They now seem silent with embarrassment,
Knowing, full well, when they go,
So too goes the silt beneath our feet.

She says,"You'll need to pay up at the bar next time,"
Then drives away.

Croppy peck at my bait.
The mosquitoes will make
A meal of me and my traveling companion,
Before I can pull my supper
From beneath these beautifully troubled waters.

David Havird

Taking Aim

"Killing varmints" was what it was for,
the brother who lives at the "hunt club" insisted. Snouts
with tusks were rooting in food plots, mauling the chufa.
After dark he'd go with the rifle, which boasted
a heat-sensing night scope. Heading out,
shot a boar at maybe fifty yards

in the hayfield. Butchered the varmint
for loins and hams, drove country miles for ice,
then towed the carcass, chained, to the bone pit. There
at the trailer across from the hayfield, taking turns,
my wife and I, gunstock to shoulder, left
arm against a utility pole to steady our aim.

No hog in sight. Merely an orange blob
like one of those mites that plague our patio's Eden,
the potted tomatoes. A deer,
that brother-in-law of mine maintained,
in killing range three football fields away,
on the opposite side, woods-fringed, of the hayfield.

Likewise deer a lethal hundred yards
across the island field where corn
was sprouting—heads when raised had necks—
a grazing pair. I handed off
the rifle, mind gone elsewhere,
stalking a buck in a poem, an archer

disentangled from sweaters, blue jeans shucked
and long johns peeled, stiff bones so cold they shine,
courting if not the embrace of the antlers
in which he may have hung as a dream
in the predawn mind of the buck, naked as now
without the frightening scent of a hunter — if not

the embrace of branches like those, for sure the embrace,
brown-leafed, of hardwoods and fir thickets' green;
matching his barefoot step to the buck's in dance
before reweaving himself in wool
that smells, retrieving longbow and arrows,
beginning to hunt. The poet, a teacher of mine,

had been at twenty an airman like God, but now,
a sometime hunter with flesh on, and lakeside home,
he tried to see with those others, homeowners too,
whose sampans he and his pilot routinely,
bombing missions accomplished,
blasted out of the water. ... Though it was dark,

darker than ever it is where streetlights hum
and neighborly lamps part curtains — neither stars
nor moon. We'd driven the farm road down through the swamp,
then up where field entangled itself in peanuts,
yonder sprouted the corn. Off to our right
the pond. (Fed by the swamp, it waters the cropland.)

Earlier, feet in leaf mulch, we'd watched from the bank,
while swatting away from our ears the whine of mosquitoes,
an alligator swimming. Tonight
against the backdrop of gum and oak
numberless fireflies, so like flashes that kill,
but not, we froze if only like children to marvel.

Hardly had shockwaves from bombs of their own,
exploding instantly, damned near knocked them unwinding
than gunfire erupted at them from the river, one
of the islands. Unheard, of course, it looked
like lightning. Those airmen scrammed,
navigator and pilot. I'd have as a child

unfrozen quickly, hands swiping,
and when there were lumens enough in the jar
(a jelly jar, nail holes in top for air),
had me a lantern . . . Play eyes too, those beetles,
like eyes outgrown that meet their grown-up gaze
and brighten. Home, the screened porch candlelit,

we're eating supper. Used to be fireflies, yes,
flashing at us from the shade of that oak?
My wife remembers while also recalling the whir:
a spray-gun-mounted truck sometimes at dusk.
The cloud that kills the mosquitoes
poisons the fireflies too.

River Trash

Crossing River Road, over the levee, to the water's edge.

Here is a tree, storm-felled, here a stained mattress with roses.

As always, when I'm home I walk off my restless sadness,
    my mother — missing.

Recliner lodged in mud. Sheet of shattered glass.

The river crosses ten states, ends downstream of New Orleans.
The deepest spot of the Mississippi is at Algiers Point,
    more than 200 feet

At the river's margin —

Paddlefish. Bluegill. Shovelnose Sturgeon.

Shredded roof shingles. Bottle of Fireball.

Crape Myrtle. Pokeweed.

I imagine dropping my body into the cold dark water in Algiers,
    then finding my mother at the river bottom.

Fork crushed in dirt. Pair of orange earbuds.

I tell myself I walk the levee because the river sharpens the world,
    river that is drift.

River a corridor for migratory birds.

Yet on my walk back to my father's house switchgrass flashes gold.

Jaw

I'll take you to the spot
where my uncle pulled
dangling from his line
a drowned human's jaw
that speckled & flapped
like a caught trout.

Black murk reflected light
that cut through leaves slashed
raw by mis-thrown fish lines
hooking bark. Further on rotted
an abandoned shanty-church
where they ladled holy water
from a yellow bucket. I'll show
you where I took the jaw
after he caught it, wiped
its slime off with my sleeve,
where I hoped the bucket,
thin with river water,
would suffice to bless
the remnant of this person,
make junk relic & wash
the sadness of this place
from our bones.

Ava Leavell Haymon

What The Magnolias Say

The postcard azaleas are over. All lavendar racemes
a month ago, wisteria's gone to bumptious vine
Pastel can't bear the heat. Winsome printemps
fragrances go north with prissy finches.
The high for the day exceeds the melting point
of light wax, and spring in Baton Rouge slumps over

into summer. The hot days
stun themselves silly with spores and dampness.
The first week in May. All the flowers are white —
ligustrum, sweet olive, jasmine up against the chainlink.
Bruised gardenias seep a coded esther, and
a padlocked door sags backwards to the Cretaceous past:
Magnolias, heaviest, whitest of all, heave open
sticky and narcotic as a sugar teat.

Harem incense streams off creamy petals,
the tarry background smell of family sins
visited on the children, of flesh sins hidden
in the linens, laced with vetivert against mildew
— dizzy whiff of hand-ripped cypress, slave-rigged
into room after room, a house bedded
on dust from a thousand overflows.
The sweetish smell of survival by any means.

It's old as sharks, this tough old plant.
Holdout from the first mother Angiosperm
who crossed seduction and pollen, made herself
a true seed, all wrapped up in itself, and bound
to change the rules of history — Moses, floated
by his sister through the simpler Nile bulrushes.

Flicker in the light: a woman's face recoils
across the whorl of petals — left to right —

vellum paging back to the beginning. The drowsy calyx
swells to fruit on the tree of knowledge.
Reach out your hand, hums the unctuous air,
potent as lithium. Take them both, male/female,
the split halves of my dicot heart.

Alison Pelegrin

Ballade on the Bogue Falaya

Having arrived fully formed, I pretended to be wild
while waiting for the others to catch up.
I chewed sassafras and stomped through creeks
confident that snakes would keep their distance.
I lost my way at midnight, out-scampered fear
on horseback while calibrating myself
to the cruel and secret company of girls,
and in this way the world passed me by.

If not Buddha, who was it who said,
of pointing at the night sky, that fingers
are words and never the moon. See how low
it hangs, and pink? I take it as a sign
to buy my Lotto ticket at this gas station here.
It feels right to hope for a Bogue Falaya refuge
with a boat docked out back to make official
the feeling of the world passing me by.

I pity cashiers who tell me to smile,
and fact checkers of the story of the life
inside of my mind, where I embellish
high points, downplay idiocy,
and ignore the burn when shame pokes through
with its dull blades. I'm stuck in a loop,
never the rogue or saint I dreamed of being,
and in this way the world passed me by.

Rarely have I found my way by the sound of water.
The days are uniform, and I wake empty-handed
on a street where all the houses look alike,
and in this way the world passed me by.

John Warner Smith

Compensation

As winter draws near, the myrtles,
bare and unassuming, stand stiffly.
Soon, they will feel the icy bitterness
of days and shadows growing shorter.
Only now do I see the distant, towering oaks,
imposing and flush with green leaves,
as their bird-nesting crowns sway
in a soft wind and reach into the clouds.
In summer, the oaks bear no bright flowers
that later fall and leave a sense of loss felt.
Their color does not mark changes
of circumstance or fate remembered.
In our mourning of death, the oaks,
timeless in endurance and grandeur,
are unseen and forgotten.
Blooms of the myrtles are reborn.

Darrell Bourque

The Dialectics of Water

I have nothing against banks or levees or towns or developers.
I have nothing against engineers & contractors & dreams. I
have no political agenda either. You know Tangipahoa &
Mermentau & Amite & the lovely people of Denham Springs,
but I am water & do not know in the ways you know. I will go
wherever I have to go, will do whatever I have to do. There
should be no blame for what cannot be blamed. I am in your
skies. I am just under the surface you call solid ground. We
live together in this place. I am in the oldest stories you tell,
in the paintings you have to paint. One day you separated from
me & began your life on a mound not me & then you began to
name things: Vermilion, Tchefuncte, & Bogue Chitto. You
called places Ticfaw, Calcasieu & Plaquemine Brûlé, Chitimacha
& Atchafalaya & Teche. Most of what you are, I am. I *inundate.*
I *gush.* I overflow & move into places. I am in your songs. I am
your basin, your delta, your backwater, your swamp, your
marsh. I am your beginning & your end.

Gina Ferrara

Living with the River

To flood, to recede
to fill each epoch, the river
wants what it wants, to meet the gulf
by cumulative, immeasurable seconds, inflicted,
infected, reluctant to heal
from a wound, a deeply given gash.
By sun and moonlight
the river is many shades
of dried blood, passing the marshes,
the mangroves, the empty estuaries,
and the barrier islands becoming less
pluralized, once lined like blades
ready to scale fish, peel citrus, and sheer cyclones.
The river deliberates and wants to shift,
to form its own opinion, to renege
on its unmade promise, a matter of course,
absent of guidance, with a telepathic current
to find and flow by fate in just the right way.

Gordon Walmsley

The River and Her Shells

The motions of the river
are silent as silt.
And there are never great waves.
Never the falling heap.
But the river can rise like Prometheus,
huge in its waking,
can break every fetter,
every encroaching restraint,
burst open
like a giant breaking irons.
And thus your stick-houses
can be swept away
when the river breaks loose
from its human prison.
You have kept me in too long,
the river might say,
have bolted me down
too much, too long.
And now I will show you
another way of breathing.
There once was a storm
that came an evening to fill the river with nightmares.
Ask her sometime about them
and she will tell you.
There is a region
between the improbable
and the unthinkable.
This is what the river told me
an evening past Easter
when the moon was drawing down.
It is a region between wakefulness
and habit, a blindspot
where eggs are lain.
Shadows of men bring them at night
and in weeks or months they hatch.
No one knows just why they are brought.
And few are they who are able to recognize
the bearers of shadows.
Yet we live in a time when shadows can be known.
Gifts of vision are upon us, if

we choose to use them.
And shadows reveal, sooner or later,
the secrets of demons.
And thus we should notice
who it is breaks the shells.
Keep the thought
and the thought will reveal itself to you.
Thus the river was able to whisper
the secrets of eggs,
brought in a night
in the twilight region
between the improbable and the unthinkable.
And yes the river felt explosions
and yes the river felt its blood, flooding
the backstreets of New Orleans
in the night a storm came
to wash away what would be washed
and to drown those who would be drowned,
both man and living things
that are part man.
The river saw a giant too
girding the whirling storm.
But the river could not tell
if the giant guided the storm,
or was merely part
of the storm's creation.
And the river wept.
For this was a terrible thing.
And we experienced the river's weeping
as rain, and thought little of it.
For it always rains.
The river knows many things
and is waiting for us to ask.
She always answers,
though she often takes her time,
for her ways are our ways.
New Orleans and her river.
The river and her New Orleans.
We take our time
interpreting the broken shells
in the time of human deeds
in the twilight region
between what is barely conceivable
and the things we would never believe.

"You cannot get through a single day without
having an impact on the world around you.
What you do makes a difference, and you have
to decide what kind of a difference you want to
make."

———————————

"If we kill off the wild, then we are killing a part
of our souls."

— Jane Goodall

"A spiritual voice is urgently needed
to underline the fact that global warming
is already causing human anguish
and mortality in our nation and abroad,
and much more will occur in the future
without rapid action."

— Bill McKibben

John Gery

Two Mississippis

for Rebecca & Darryl

I

If the river is a woman who awakens
and splashes morning in her eyes, who stretches
her arms and dips them in the dance of dawn,
then combs her hair with sunlight, as she turns
and twists to listen to the brush of trees
beside her in the early breeze, who hums
and dresses delicately, easing her limbs
into her dappled skirt, her mottled sleeves,
who sips her tea then glides out to the gate
to greet the traffic passing there, and who
on entering the street begins to stray
a little, just a little (unaware
the obstacles her independent means
impose on those who'd rather she remain
inside and watch her flowers grow, not slow
their swollen progress to some venal shore),
then bends and wanders, when the weather's right,
and reaches toward the south, and, reaching, dreams
the dreams inspiring others drifting by
to catch her sparkle, taste her sigh, or slip
behind her gaze to swim inside,

                                            then who
are we? Her lover stealing from her bed,
deserting her with lies? Her child who,
ignoring how he's sucked her dry, sucks harder?
Her god?

II

And if the river is a man
rugged and brown, but round and muscular,
who wanders through the wilderness at dusk,
who plucks a fallen branch, then ambles on
between the trees, bowing and rising, who
at coming to a clearing scales a rock,
pausing briefly, rubbing his sides, then hums
and winds around the hills to wander down
into the pine grove on their farther side,
who feeds the beetles, beavers, birds, and bears
thinking him kind, who veers through twilit shadows,
their brilliance like a memory that flashes
and is gone, who tells himself those stories
that echo in the breeze they're carried on,
whose grey eyes pool when he beholds the sun
at last, and at the last who spreads his arms
to seize its light, then turns to go alone
once more in darkness, leaving in his wake
no sign of wandering there,
                              then who are we,
waiting in silence near his path, who strike,
then leave him on the forest floor for dead?
Are we, earth's thieves, so starved that we must bleed
the bled? Can no kind words for us be said?

Julie Kane

Purple Martin Suite

"I had several opportunities, at the period of their arrival, of seeing prodigious flocks moving over [New Orleans] or its vicinity, at a considerable height. ... I walked under one of them with ease for upwards of two miles, at that rate on the 4th of February 1821, on the bank of the river below the city, constantly looking up at the birds, to the great astonishment of many passengers, who were bent on far different pursuits." — John James Audubon

1.
Any excuse, a holiday or death
will make them twirl umbrellas, shake their butts
to brass band music in the streets. I swear,
what won't these people make a party of?
So when my neighbor loaded beer on ice
and grabbed two folding chairs and said he meant
to go watch birds roost underneath a bridge,
it seemed no odder an excuse than Lent
to celebrate. We parked the pickup truck
by Entergy and slid down dirt banks under
girders where the Causeway Bridge meets land,
silenced by the rush-hour traffic's thunder
whizzing overhead. No sign, yet, of a bird.
I had to take my neighbor at his word.

2.
I had to take my neighbor at his word
that there would be a show, as birds arrived
in ones and twos and then in blue-black streams
from day locations up to thirty miles
in all directions, by my neighbor's math.
This was the staging ground for their migration
southward, down the Gulf of Mexico,
to the far corners of the Amazon Basin:
bridgeworks to rest on and clouds of mosquitoes
ripe for the sunset-plucking on this lake
where no one sane would build a city (floods
& yellow fever), let alone then take
the scraps left over and build backyard homes
for birds that can't build shelters on their own.

3.
For birds that can't build shelters on their own
we'd gathered, half a dozen of us there.
At first the martins flew at random, making
meaningless blue-black scribbles on the air,
thousands and thousands of them swarming; then,
as if an orchestra were tuning up,
the sun dipped under the horizon like
the fall of a baton, the "theater" hushed,
and suddenly the birds began to soar
in perfect loop-de-loops and barrel rolls,
whole squadrons of them flying synchronized
as vintage prop planes in an aircraft show,
till even those not mystically inclined
would swear they were connected mind to mind.

4.
As if they were connected mind to mind,
one group of them broke off and swooped en masse
below the Causeway, settling wing to wing
along steel girders; then a second pass,
a third, as any birds who hadn't found
a spot the last dive, flowed into the next,
the way a mother braids a daughter's hair
or villanelle picks up old lines of text.
When they were finished it was way too dark
to tell their outlines from the sky or lake.
We stood and clapped as if we'd seen the Meters
reunited on a Jazz Fest stage,
joined beat to beat and holding in our breath
as night fell on that holiday from death.

Jack B. Bedell

Ghost Swell, Henderson

"Find beauty, be still." — W.H. Murray

This swamp never stops breathing.
　　　Find shade somewhere
　　　　　and string up a hammock.

Close your eyes. The bug whine
　　　dips and swells, water
　　　　　laps against the roots

of trees. You'll learn to hear
　　　distance, the sharp flaps
　　　　　of wings. Quiet your mind

and you may even pick out
　　　claws scratching down cypress bark.
　　　　　Keep at this until the sun

drops past the tree line and you'll
　　　feel the hum of spirits
　　　　　gathering on the lake's surface.

Remember, you are always free
　　　to linger here. Just be still.
　　　　　Mind your beating heart.

*Henderson is located in St. Martin Parish, off the I-10 on the edge of
the Atchafalaya Basin swamp, just east of Lafayette.*

III

Louisiana Pines

Gentle rolling highways through
Northwest corner, near the toes of the Ozark foothills
To the marshy toes of the boot-shaped state,
Host to cultures with unexpected wonders.

Acres of standing pines
Singing a river song in soft breeze,
The pounding of mechanical pumps on gulf waters
Pulling oil from primordial depths,
Singing a different song than those
Who fish the salty waters and
Chank-a-chank in a different language.

Pining for the old days
Before those sounds were known.
When pelicans filled the sky and
Seagulls shouted joyful finds of
Fish schools too vast to measure,

When Grand Isle's shoreline was
Not yet dotted with platforms,
Christmas tree lights, and natural gas torches
Reaching thirty feet above the horizon,

When marshland covered itself in
Vibrant colors of migrating flocks,
Wings slapping salty humid air,
When my father and his father before
Had only one care —
That day's catch.

Catching now the scent of pine,
I remember his face as he retold
From childhood memory how
Plentiful our *cadie* once was
Before Louisianians pined.

Ava Leavell Haymon

Changing Weather Patterns

El Niño slips across latitudes, rises dripping from the ocean
From seafloor mud, El Niño brings up the secrets of childhood
El Niño crawls in the manger, time runs out
El Niño rocks himself dry on the edge of a continent
Prairies of wheat go unpollinated, there is rumor
El Niño is killing the honeybees

The water turns cold, La Niña follows her twin
Windowpanes darken, the weather channel shows us rain
Angels proclaim in vain above unseasonal cloud cover
La Niña lines up her hurricanes in alphabetical order
Floodwaters announce her coming   The rich bribe airlines
while the poor push children into branches of trees

The Niños hear their names on the news in every language
The Niños bankrupt distant cities with mudslides
Comets snuff out in dirty skies   Celebrities seduce us
away from the guides in our dreams   Lovers of chaos,
computers roll back their zero eyes   The trumpet cries
Los Niños in a loud voice   Faces on billboards draw closer

La Niña, we pray, and El Niño, her brother
We long for sweetness and scale
Our tables sag under piles of unsorted papers
Spare us, Niños   We don't know winter from summer
Above the trade winds, ozone crackles
their answer: We have come for the children

Apocalypse

September 2005

New Orleans, awash in broken melodies,
Bucktown's levee nearly did you in, the lake
bleeding-in to reveal you. Thus you have become
apocalyptic, for apocalypse means
laying bare what was hidden.
And as in any apocalypse
a mirror is held up
to every single one of us.
I imagine sharks coming in for the dead
or an alligator's eyes
bobbing the waters of Bayou St. John.
All that was hidden
rising to the surface. Scrutiny
from the Cotswolds
to the China Sea.

And what in you is brought to light
may change this stumbling nation.

We who were born of you always knew
there was a beast sleeping heavily below.
We could sometimes hear it breathing at night
or sense its faint smell when the wind was wrong.
We knew too, only the lake's blood could rouse it
and free us from its dreaming
so that then we could be led
to the intimate place of mirrors.

Jordan Biggs

What Once Was

when i was a child the marsh stretched out for miles
how beautiful it was to see from a flat boat
but my childhood is gone
as is much of the marsh

this community calls me a fool
for i believe irreversibly damaging our marsh
is unforgivable
it's tainted
it's poisoned
some believe what is told by corporations
that the marsh was made for carbon sequestration
and LNG is the future of louisiana
that this is our only option
to turn wetlands into wastelands

yes, at least there's still some orange groves
the ones that used to stretch to the levee
in fields that stretched for miles
but now the groves only go back a few rows
just like the marsh
both nearly dead now
yet those who remember,
who refuse to forget
will plant new seeds
and tomorrow orange trees might thrive again

but, sadly, today the marsh screams for help
and though only a few of us can hear — or care
i sit by the marsh and we softly cry together

Double Crossed

A guy walks into a wilderness, gets lost,
Exhausted, then still more lost, keeps walking.
Sun begins to set. He battles panic.
The woods get very dark.
Might as well be without a flashlight in a cave.

The next day, he starts walking again
Never having slept, but walks nowhere,
No trail of any kind to follow anywhere,
No waterways or distant mountains,
To let him know where he's going.
He keeps walking, the green scenery
Never changing, morning same
As afternoon, both as hopeless
As night's complete shadow.

At last, a marker — he sees a set of sticks
Crossed just so, senses some intelligence
Must have put these here, stunned to think
That same entity could still be nearby,
Perhaps eyeing him right now, about
To pounce — terror then splits him in two
Like lightning hitting a tree, so he races off
Nowhere, the dread of some other mind

Blanking his mind, though that other mind
Just a mirror of his own, detached,
Abstract, all his mind able to hold.
He runs, runs but figures it follows him,
A shadow, and so wheeling around,
Seeing nothing, he throws himself down
And begins to claw at the ground,
To burrow, to hunker into a bunker,
The entrance hidden by a make-believe
Garden, where he grows his make-believe
Food, the garden hidden by a high wall
Of actual brush he piled up, camouflaged
In the vast green, masked and, he hopes,

Unseen.

But he must have run in a circle
Because peering out of his lair
Soon after he got it all set just so,
He sees his underground edifice
Hard upon that original X that marked
The spot that first loosed the dread
That some other had set a trap, sparked
His flight and that now marks the spot
Where he has buried his treasure, his life.

Frozen now, his terror becomes
Despair and never again does
He come back out, just burrows
Further and further and further down.
Before long he starves, and over time
The walls begin to crumble and collapse
On his remains, and the wilderness reclaims
It all, swallowing back into the vast green
The last trace of his ever having been there,
Even the crossed sticks, at last, all gone.

His mask became his tomb.
No monstrous horror though, no shame —
Every life plays out this same way.
The entire green vastness, every tree, leaf,
And shrub telling versions of the same tale
In reaching toward the sun, laughing off
The folly, the false knowledge, the double self
Their forked tongues sang into nowhere
But farther down into the ground, delighted
Now to be growing back up together
As a vast expanse of undifferentiated green.

Andy Young

Deepwater Horizon

April 2010

Take a deep breath, I say to myself,
but must beware the petroleum wind,
the spreading slick, rig workers blasted and sent
to bones and wreckage in the Gulf
now gushing plumes from the mantle's wealth.
The wellhead swells and looses filth.
Each tide is slick with thick, sweet crude.
It etches delicate marshes and blends

Benzene with oyster brine. Across
the coast, useless yellow booms afloat,
fishing nets hang slack with loss.
The earth will not die, though it
might shrug off a continent,
convert and re-form us: fossil and dross.

How to Wash a Duck

1. A soft scarf secures the bill, firm hands of a striptease artist.

2. Ignore the stifled quacks emitted through the muffled bill.

3. A second pair of gloved hands must hold the flapping wings closed.

4. Allow the tail feathers to wiggle, bounce, and dance like Donald Duck forgetting to be mad. Even in frustration a hunk of fluff, a bouncing duck butt swaying from side to side makes right in the world.

5. Begin and end with two webbed, leathery feet. A holy act is to wash a duck's feet.

6. Scrub soap on the pretty part of the mallard's wings. The ocean and the bird's teal feathers shine as slick oil slips away.

7. Use the same dish soap on these precious oil-slathered birds as the brand you use at home. *Palmolive, much better than Dove,* as the TV lady used to say.

8. Hope that after the scrub and rinse, only the duck's natural oil remains, protective of man's messy disaster.

9. Apologize for spilled oil polluting an entire habitat, marsh, ocean, and earth. The duck doesn't care if it's his fault, my fault, or yours. Offer a duck a prayer. Whisper it to anyone who cares to hear.

10. Release the restless, chatty bill, watch the duck waddle, exit a blanketed crate, then freedom.

Ashley Mace Havird

Ghost Net

Breeze-thrown seafoam,
breakers and swells . . .
The deep moans round
with many voices ...
Stampedes of storms that fail
to rouse a soul, or so it seems,
to dead zones, red tides,
coral bleached to bone.
Whales — huge, confused —
heave ashore.

Beneath fever-laced blankets
of carbon, tributaries heavy
with fertilizer, pesticide,
industrial sludge — a riot of dreams.
Dynamite and cyanide,
longlines and trawling net,
gill, tangle, and drift net;
sweat-drenched dreams
of taking.

Leavings.
Mooring ropes, frayed, barnacled,
lash the oily shores of the Gulf.
Fishing lines knot
sea fans, sargassum, strap algae,
turtle grass — knot them
into bouquets, ceremonial decay.
Ghost nets,
forgotten by fishermen,
ride the waves, ripe
with rotting bycatch
and plastic — turtles, toothbrushes,
dolphins, flip-flops. Casting
and reeling its tides,
the sea aims
to hook open our eyes,
or so I might believe
if the living sea meant anything.

Bill Lavender

Grand Isle

All along Caminada Pass now the rip-rap
is unbroken, stone wall between the unrelenting
waves of the western Gulf and the delicate
southwest point of the island. The chenière
that rooted the ground on this end was swept
away by Katrina, leaving a small acre of sea
oats now being trampled by backhoes
and dump trucks. They have covered the beach
with rubber for a good way there
and laid out great canvas socks of sand
to reinforce the levee, and time will
tell how these hi-tech measures work.

How long before this island, the big island,
dissolves back into the sea like the
Chenière Caminada? Islands like people
are of finite duration, especially these
alluvial mounds of pure sand, accretions
of humus and glass dropped by the river
built up by the waves and finally pulled down
by those same waves. One
would need to be as mobile as a bird
to nest on one, and I suppose we are,
these extravagant camps periodically
reduced to piles of sticks by the storms
while their owners worry back in New Orleans
or Baton Rouge or Lafayette, and old
bare pilings stand around Caminada Bay
like remnants of Spanish language in the argot.

*Grand Isle has a central ridge several feet above sea level which is called a chenier,
derived from the French for "oak ridge." Unlike other barrier islands in the Gulf the
chenier allowed for growth of extensive oak groves whose roots provided a livable land.*

Playground for the rich ever since they
cut the canal and boat service opened,
home of second homes for French
Quarter traders, where wives and children
might summer, and then the big shot
of oil money mid-20th century that brought
the entire matrix of rigs and refineries
and canals, dredging the passes to keep
the equipment moving.

Insatiate the next morning I went down
into the surf early, walked the 50 yards
out to the sandbar and stood knee deep
throwing a gold spoon. The day was
slightly overcast and the sunrise stunning.
Porpoises breached in the light chop and
mullet swarmed on the surface. An hour
yielded me two keeper specks, enough
for supper at least, and I waded in absently
with my stringer. The surf was frothing
just at shoreline and I saw within it
a five-foot tiger shark, the dorsal and tail
and even the bare back well visible over the
foot-deep foam and close enough I could
have tapped him with my pole. I froze and
watched him calmly pass, first shark
I had seen on the beach, and then from
the safety of the sand watched him make
his round, westward down the beach
always hiding in the froth, then out into
the channel and back east, fins breaking
surface now and then making
a dotted line of his progress.

*1805 to 1814 were the pirate years for the area when Jean Lafitte and his privateers
were based on nearby Grand Terre. They raided mostly Spanish ships for "black ivory"
(slaves) and other booty to be resold in New Orleans.*

We go out early evening, Nanc having
scoffed at my fear of the shark, and from
the sandbar hook a couple which get away.
One is a Spanish Mackerel which jumps
insanely when hooked, leaping six feet
out of the water, flipping himself off the hook
before I can get a net under him. We plot
an early morning return to the lagoon with
the kayaks. I'm mad at her because she came
out without her shirt and no amount of sun-
screen will protect you completely. It's six
o'clock she says, and I ask what difference
that makes since the sun is still high in the
sky. We hear a splash and look to my right
just in time to see the shark thrashing with
something on the surface 100 feet from us.
"I'm going in," I say, and she follows.

At house built in the 1930s, with an old oak tree,
we pack the kayaks on the truck that very
evening so we can just get up and go
and eat breakfast later. No need to set
an alarm; I wake up at 5 and we are
launching the kayaks by 6. The redfish
cut the water all around but still
refuse to bite anything we show them.
I row around trolling with my spoon,
try bait living and dead, a sparkle beetle:
nothing.

The 1893 hurricane killed 2000 people along the Gulf Coast but Grand Isle fared better;
however, the island has been hit hard by numerous hurricanes, including Katrina (2005),
yet it has always found a way to rebuild.

Finally, all the way at the end
where a short rock jetty separates the lagoon
from Barataria Pass, something bites my
spoon and I land it. It is not a fish I have
ever seen before. Perch-shaped but meatier,
small mouth, it looks suspiciously like a
bass except for an overall reddish tint.
The eyes are wild, yellowish red around
the pupils. I keep it, even though I don't
know what it is, and later catch two more.
I get out and walk the rocks, like the proverb-
ial cow, fishing the gulf side. I get
hung in the rocks and lose one rig, two.
I land one speck and then, to my great
surprise, on a spoon, a nice little flounder.*

*This poem was written just a few years after Hurricane Katrina and the Deepwater
Horizon oil spill. Prior to these two disasters (both, in different ways, human-caused) we
could catch ice-chests-full of speckled trout and redfish in the surf there. The paucity of
our catch on this trip indicates the long-lasting decline in the fish population at Grand
Isle, formerly one of the most diverse and productive estuaries on Earth.

Alison Pelegrin

As I Stand on a Paddle Board for the First Time in June, I Plan for October's Eclipse

after James Wright

Knowing full well the folly
of counting on tomorrow, I resolve
to be on Bayou Castine
for the eclipse coming in 100 days.
I've got solar glasses and a flashlight
to wear around my neck,
and I'll pack a flask, because if you're not
reading boat names and sipping bourbon
on the bayou during the total eclipse,
why even bother?

But now it is summer,
and I live for darkness where it is cooler,
roaming the yard in board shorts and Crocs.
How do I, who barely have
my balance, dare dream of gliding
among cypress stoic in black waters?
Tonight's crickets salute the thunder moon.
Those that will sing their confusion
to the future have just taken root.

Martha Serpas

Ten Fathom Ledge

All that's visible
      is a ribbon of coral,
briny phrasals above a ledge nearly

erased by silt and scalloped water,
      ghostly and opaque.

Beyond is the dead outer shelf,
its tragic red surge of blossoms
      bruising the abyss.

What to do?
      The others have entered

the freighter's wrenched hull,
their light beams sliding like opera gloves
along the awkward deck and sides.

I am left playing with goatfish
      on Ten Fathom Ledge, the forbidden
step off your grandmother's porch,
the first plank as far as you will go
toward the long bright yard, the pitch
      of children rippling from a swing.

Why not be content with spadefish and nurse sharks,
      the confusion of gravity, the wise bezel
that grasps all our time as bottom time?
A gentle surge toward the wreck lifts, pauses,
      then sloshes me right back on the ledge.

Everything lasts forever: the jetties,
      sand, sky, pipers, even the pebbles
of sea glass, cobalt, old as lace
doilies. Others can walk down the beach
toward thin shacks and driftwood shelters,

toward haze and mist. I'll sit on an unclaimed
      log, which has drifted here, for now,
and watch a midday sun crystal
on the waves. Don't be fooled:

The Gulf is not a polished cruiser
      or a V-hull on the dock.

The Gulf
      is not a flatiron idling
between sets of bowing waves.

Its striated water lifts itself inch by inch
and closes in on the shore.
                     It is alive,
playing its chords, humming its undertow.

You will be welcomed on your back
as it slides its dress collar over
      your thighs, runs its breezes and tensions
all over you. It will welcome your face floating down,
closed eyes or open, as it breathes
      August's strong sweat.
It will welcome you a thousand times.
It wants you to practice sinking
         and feel how much you belong.

Others can walk the shore's silver brocade
      and pace back again.

Don't be fooled: The sky is complicit.
      There's no discerning compass here.
The wings and water pull equally
      toward the beauty of transparence —
      cirri, sea fans, music, love

and the pans and stirrups of pelicans
which weigh that anything is possible,
      but that nothing has to be.

Julia Johnson

Chenière Caminada

We see it
form a terrible trough
and hear that ringing
we have been told about.
We hold a map and we
know where the northwest
Caribbean Sea is. We think
of the sky as a hood. We walk across
rice fields and wade in calm, cold water.
We walk between orange trees.
We watch the shrimp cannery slipping and tilting
into the water. The trees bend.
We hear the waves in the evening.
We fall beneath the magnifying surge.
We come up, hold onto a fence, move in mud.
We wait for a day in a church with the priest
and a light, read a book on United States presidents.

The hurricane of 1893 devastated the island of Chenière Caminada (west of Grand Isle), killing many of the island's 1,500 inhabitants. Prior to that the 4-mile-long fishing village had been a diverse community, with a Catholic church. Residents provided oysters, shrimp and oranges to markets upriver.

Sue Owen

When Pelicans Cannot Fly

Yes, they were born brown
but that doesn't mean
they like to bathe in oil.
That doesn't mean they like

To nest near the toxic brew
or like to smell its stink.
Oil doesn't mix well with
water, and neither does it

suit the brown pelicans,
who must eat their fish
basted in oil and swallow
the whole mess in one gulp.

What must the pelicans
be thinking of us now,
when they cannot fly, must
perch alone on their islands,

their heads hunched back
on their shoulders, their
pouches tucked in, their
long bills at rest on

their chests, because they
cannot fly, swim, or eat, so
they eye us and their death?
And when their feathers

have turned this brown
from the oil and their soaked
wings can no longer glide,
who can answer that stare?

Lament the Owl

Lament the osprey
Lament the pelican, covered in oil
Life is narrow
Thin like a line of blue light
Pulled through a hole in a needle
We enter the needle
Briefly sewn to a blouse of living
Growing up to mend the world
Lament the owl
Lament the osprey
Lament the pelican dressed in oil
We are cornered
The choices are slim
Reach out and offer a hand of assistance
Wash the owl
Apologize to the osprey
Pray for the pelican
We are trapped
Wanting so much
We did not consider
The needs of the osprey

Note: Pollution in one part of the food chain, such as in fish, affects other parts.

Michael S. True

The Very Air We Breathe

Don't be afraid
It's the flavor of the day
This reticent scent
An olfactory factor
Meant to trigger alarm
Avoidance imperative
A hesitance to inhale
For the sake of the brain
An aversion to death
Cued by wrinkled nose
And gasping breath
Burning lungs to sound the siren
Perhaps a little too late
As with smoke and fire
Oxygen is the first to be displaced
This cruel asphyxia stealing away
The very essence of life
Our fate to suffocate before the flame
So too the petrol-smog conspiracy
To coat the lungs
Choke us like our old friend agent orange
The last roundup
A matter of particulates
Wind, water, soil, sun
The dust of the drought
An asthmatic flood
What is that smell?
Can't tell if it's
Methane or skunk
And of course
All the unscented air
That swirls around out there

It hardly seems fair
That some chemists
Have spared our collective noses
Hiding their poisons
In the scent of roses
Or in aerosols that don't happen to stink
Death hiding in lethal clouds
Threatening everything and everyone
Chemical attacks to be disavowed
Now, the mind's on the brink
This panic to think
That we may never truly know
What evil lurks in the very air we breathe

Trashscape Girlhood

Trashy, worthless first attested 1620 —

At the river E and I smoke my mother's cigarettes   rope swing
   barge our trusted landscape

It's the morning after we watch *The Day After*   movie we were
   told not to see alone

We don't discuss it.

Are two girls not safe alone at the edge of a river?

How to think about the word *rot*, I might consider much later.

Let's go back and imagine bodies on fire, melting, the world
   gone nuclear.

Or the sky above the Mississippi, waxy, color of turned milk.

Or also the river, slick with green and fever bright.

Childhood for us was a flicker, a sting? Not a melting.

Gone nuclear — is this a chance to be very angry?

Seep and leak.

Are two girls not safe?

How the Cold War starts and continues.

Meanwhile what would it mean to be *trashy*: Too much makeup?
   Dirty hair? Splintered fingernails?

What would it mean to be radioactive?

Gone nuclear?

Yes once again, how a woman is turned *trash* by virtue of
     a short skirt.

At the edge.

How we tally   how in the movie we learn about body counts
     radiation   bomb blooming
over and over in slow motion   we are reckless girls who know
     the world is ending

How we are girls ready for fall-out and no shelter

We are girls who don't trust ourselves because we have been
     taught not to.

How my high school teacher made me read
the first paragraph of *Lolita* out loud to him alone
     in a dark room.

Leak. Tally. Count.

How many years till the end of the earth.

A bomb blooming.

Why would we trust? And who?

My teacher? Our mothers?

E and I blow smoke rings, climb the levee's edge, dizzy with heat,

and should we not love the easy promise
of the world's end
we half-believe in?

Cancer Alley

(To a quick mock-martial tempo)

Welcome here to Cancer Alley
Where Death lives and thrives at a fixed address
With a fatal gallop, in glittering dress
It combs the streets to boost its tally

Landfill Lane, Toxic Dump Crescent
A boon from business, a mighty present
A puff of profit, the fantastic bribe
We're the Dead End dwellers, the chosen tribe

We drink our water, laced with lead
In our speck of dust a ton of dioxin
We live and die like yoked-up oxen
Oh how so blessed to be sorely bled!

There's a reddish vapour from my bedroom floor
From the frightened wall a yellow ooze
The Government Inspector discerns no flaw
Should the tenants move there's a lot to lose

Highway 10 is above my roof
The railtrack splits my blessed garden
For my deafened ears I need no proof
The music of my life is eternal din

A chemical plant blooms by my fence
My breath is a fare of fumes and smokes
A battered warrior without defence
My heart is a rubble of stress and strokes

Here's the Coughing Cradle, the Asthma Country
The cracked-up kidney, the wasted liver
Lungs perforated like a riddled reefer
In the Dead End Zone, what a blissful bounty!

Pause

Three-fingered hands two-headed babies one-legged frog birds with missing wings fatal floods vengeful droughts hole in the sky hole in the sky hole in the sky in the sky hole in the sky the river caught fire hole in the sky the river caught fire hole in the sky in the sky in the sky hole in the . . .

Pause

Welcome here to Cancer Street
The City's Waste Dump, and its pitch-Black death
They punch our sky, hazard our health
The earth is fire beneath our feet

Terra Bianca

Terra Bianca® is an imaginary color
of not-wood that decorates my space.
It is the gray shade of coastal ghost forests,
salt-poisoned stands of once-cypress
haunting our manufactured coast.

Fitting for this business of oil and chemical
tanks, the miles of pipe stretched out like
a leviathan's fossil skeleton unearthed,
dinosaur oil and all its products
flowing into the river and the sea.

Our darkest oil fuels the tankers which blow
their stacks in blossoming clouds of soot,
hoping no one will notice in the Black towns
of the old plantation road called Cancer Alley.
Gas flares metastasize excess methane

so as to bring about the dinosaurs' revenge
of catastrophic weather. Their feathered descendants
fall from the sky exhausted, searching for the vanished
marsh in which their parents nested, replaced
by open water dotted with the heads of wells.

The skeletal remains of this office will stand someday
in open water, the Terra Bianca cabinetry
hanging from the rusted bones and tangled
copper neurons, another monument warning:
look on my works, survivors, and despair!

Martha Serpas

Crossing

Out on the open water, finally, they see all
        seven deltas and their depositions,
mouth bars and inlets

running like childhood scars across the coast.

All night while the shrimp run
        and into the next hot day,
the last generation sits on Igloos

picking shrimp, following those before them
        till the nets are empty, passing the time
coaxing loggerheads close while bored porpoises

drift, with no wake to spin.

A certain quiet fills the hull
        for a proper discernment
of the shore, a certain sweat while they scan

for the new order of things,
        which is the old order renewed, things

moving swiftly but weighed immovable
        in their eyes. Someone might forget
to declare "good" or "very good" or "evil"

as they drift among their last breaths, their burials,
        and this third idle death that frees the soul's
wisdom, still ignorant of its crossing.

Who knows what God will breathe out
        after our last breath is drawn?

Some might see estuaries that unite
          the brackish bath and fluvial birth,
sandy islands that split the tide,

cypresses both gasping the bank and stretching
          their slender shadows on the channel

when God remembers the interstice
          of our muddy ossuary and our exhalations —
cordgrass and bulrush, bulltongue
and shellfish, sawgrass and maidencane —

a white coast of grass and salt and dragonflies.

Friends: Don't seal me in a marble card catalog
          to which no borrowers come.
Let the ferry go without me. Let me join
          the trawlers and gather my broad nets alone.

The Golden Rule of Water

> "Do unto those downstream as you
> would have those upstream do unto you."
> — Wendell Berry

Keep it safe. Keep it pure.
Keep it clean — because this is a family establishment
and we're all one of the children.
Keep it flowing.
Keep it wet, because sooner or later, all of us get dry.
Keep it clear, so we can see to the bottom of things,
so we can see our own reflections in the surface
or what we'll be getting ourselves into if we dive.
Keep it aquifer. Keep it spring.
Keep it a well worth wishing into.
Keep it puddle, pond, creek, stream,
lake, river, ocean — one and many.
Keep it rain.
Keep it free.
Keep it abundant — or at least
keep it enough,
because while water has reportedly been turned
into wine, I've never heard tell of even Jesus
turning things back again.
Keep it oil and water don't mix
and we don't want our rainbows in the gutters, but the sky.
So, keep it you take your share, I'll take mine.
Keep it ours and everyone's.
Keep it. Because it's all we got.

Peter Cooley

Matters of Difference

The difference between poetry and prayer
is just the difference between sea and sky,
between this jade plant my wife bought for me
after I told her one would always sprawl
beside me in the public library
where I first opened books which spelled a world
and driving Mississippi whose forests
countless are the cosmos Columbus caught
and catching, lost and we are still losing.
I want to say this more precisely now —
I don't know how — body is where it starts,
soul were it stops. In medieval debates
as they argue, this always stands unsaid.
One dies, the other lives eternally
but without life there's no eternity.
There's no sky without all the muck down here.

For the Hardest Days

Some evenings, after days when the world feels
like it has poured all of its despair into me,
when I am awash with burdens that rests atop
my body like a burlap of jostling shadows,

I find a place to watch the sun set. I dig
my feet into a soil that has rebirthed itself
a million times over. I listen to the sound
of leaves as they decide whether or not

it is time to descend from their branches.
It is hard to describe the comfort one feels
in sitting with something you trust will always be
there, something you can count on to remain

familiar when all else seems awry. How remarkable
it is to know that so many have watched the same
sun set before you. How the wind can carry
pollen and drop it somewhere it has never been.
How the leaves have always become the soil

that then become the leaves again. How maybe
we are not so different from the leaves.
How maybe we are also always being reborn
to be something more than we once were.

How maybe that's what waking up each morning is.
A reminder that we are born
of the same atoms as every plant and bird
and mountain and ocean around us.

Ralph Adamo

My Poem in Which Hope Exists

Just to be alive on earth and walk down to the water
Just to have the sound of it in your ears, and to wish
Food in the bellies of all the earth's people, now, and whenever
They are hungry. Such a simple place, earth, if we subtract
The worst things in each of our hearts, if we become
Generous in the same way trees are, giving away everything
While standing firm not indifferent to color or light but
Taking them in the friendly hug of time and space until
The thing earth wants from us, our sharp minds in service
Our hands working but able to rest and the breath of billions
Exhaling easily in the evening breeze in the heart of the home
      we share
Should share in equal measure and with no further rancor
Drawn by water, made one with the waters wandering ways
Whole like new like each and all births renew us and we keep

Jack B. Bedell

New Beach, Elmer's Island
— Caminada Headlands, 2018

Before they brought this beach back
  with barge after barge of sand

scraped out of the Mississippi's delta,
  the island had melted to a thin strip

of grass where waves broke hard
  on their way to chew mainland coast.

No headland buffer to slow down
  the Gulf's salt water, no room to walk,

nowhere for cranes to nest — this place
  was a hyperlapse of loss, a door

not so much unlocked as off its hinges
  and left to rot away. Now, though,

acres of shore sprawl against the Gulf,
  full of shore birds. Tall dunes

ready the island for the water's hot rise,
  storms sure to come. One island

cannot stop the sinking inland,
  or put back cemeteries and roadways

washed away by tide, but it can
  buy us time. And all time is hope.

Elmer's Island is located just west of Grand Isle. It's a Wildlife Refuge that still rewards the adventuresome with recreational fishing, bird watching and eco-education.

Notes on Contributors

Ralph Adamo — native New Orleanian poet; author of *All the Good Hiding Places*, *All Fall Down*, *Evermore*, and *Waterblind*; editor at *Xavier Review*.

Randy Bates — taught writing at the University of New Orleans for several years; author of *Rings: On the Life and Family of a Southern Fighter*.

Grace Bauer — former resident of New Orleans; taught creative writing at the University of Nebraska; author of *Unholy Heart*, *The Women at the Well*, *Nowhere All At Once*, *Retreats and Recognitions*, and *Beholding Eye*. She now lives in Philadelphia, Pennsylvania.

Jack B. Bedell — coordinator of the Creative Writing program at Southeastern Louisiana University. Poet Laureate of Louisiana (2017–2019); editor at *Louisiana Literature*; author of *Against the Woods' Dark Trunks*, *Ghost Forest* (Mercer University Press), *No Brother, This Storm*, and *Color All Maps New*.

Steve Beisner — originally from Pointe Coupe Parish; computer science graduate of M.I.T.; writer of short stories and poems. Commutes between Louisiana and California.

Jordan Biggs — a Gen Z writer whose family lost their home in Buras, Louisiana, during Hurricane Katrina. Her Cajun roots and love of the Lower Mississippi River Delta inspire many of her poems.

Darrell Bourque — Louisiana Poet Laureate (2007–2011); author of *The Blue Boat*, *In Ordinary Light*, *Megan's Guitar*, *Burnt Water* and *Until We Talk*.

Maxine Cassin — poet and publisher (New Orleans Poetry Journal Press); author of *Turnip's Blood*, *The Other Side of Sleep*, and *Against the Clock*. Because of their friendship, she was able to incorporate stunning photographs by Clarence J. Laughlin into her work.

Kellie Considine — grew up in Pennsylvania where she often played in nature; she earned an MBA at the University of Kentucky and she now lives and writes in New Orleans.

Nicole Cooley — poet who grew up in New Orleans; author of seven books of poems, including *Mother Water Ash*, *Girl After Girl After Girl* and *Breach* (all LSU Press). Her new collection, *Trash*, is forthcoming from Alice James Books. She teaches at Queens College, City University of New York.

Peter Cooley — director of creative writing at Tulane University (1975–2018); Louisiana Poet Laureate (2015–2017). His collections include: *The Astonished Hours*, *Sacred Conversations*, *A Place Made of Starlight*, *Divine Margins*, and *The One Certain Thing*.

Michael Czarnecki — well-traveled poet and publisher (Foothills Press); author of *Never Stop Asking for Poems*, *Simple Life, Simple Poems*, and *Sea Smoke and Sand Dollars*; as a publisher he spearheaded an important ecological collection titled *The Dire Elegies*.

Toby Daspit — teaches in the Education Department at the University of Louisiana at Lafayette; author of *Bar Coasters*, *Anatomy of a Ghost,* and a forthcoming collection. He has also served as the Emeritus Consultant for the National Writing Project of Acadiana.

Charles deGravelles — writes poetry, fiction, and nonfiction; author of *The Well Governed Son*; his work is included in *Uncommon Place: An Anthology of Contemporary Louisiana Poets* (LSU Press); he also penned a biography, *Billy Cannon: A Long, Long Run.*

Dean Ellis — poet; translator (of Jacinto Lucas Pire's novel *The True Actor*, with Jaime Braz); radio show host ("Tudo Bem" and "The Dean's List") at WWOZ-FM; and author of the poetry book *Far Flung* (Portals Press).

Malaika Favorite — visual artist and poetic writer, her publications include *Dreaming at the Manor, Illuminated Manuscript, Ascension* (poems), *The Author Project* (novella), and *After Color* (novel, 2025).

Gina Ferrara — Louisiana Poet Laureate (2025—); author of *Ethereal Avalanche, AMISS, Amber Porch Light,* and other works. She has also hosted The Poetry Buffet at the Latter Library in New Orleans for several years.

Mark Folse — longtime roots in South Louisiana; studied in the MFA creative writing program at the University of New Orlean; widely published in anthologies, including in *The Maple Leaf Rag*.

Dennis Formento — editor and publisher of *Mesechabe*, a journal of environmental writings; studied poetics at Naropa (Boulder, Colorado); author of *Spirit Vessels*. Lives in the watershed of the West Pearl River.

Joan M. Garvey — painter (especially watercolor) and photographer (especially while birdwatching); member of Orleans Audubon Society.

John Gery — creative writing professor at the University of New Orleans; author of *A Gallery of Ghosts, Have at You Now, Davenport's Version,* and *The Enemies of Leisure*. He directs the Ezra Pound Center.

Ashley Mace Havird — Shreveport-based poet; author of *Wild Juice* (LSU Press), *The Garden of the Fugitives,* and *Lightningstruck* (a novel). She was the Caddo Parish Poet Laureate from 2018–2021.

David Havird — widely published poet; taught many years at Centenary College; author of *Weathering*.

Ava Leavell Haymon — poet, playwright, writing teacher, and editor; served as Louisiana Poet Laureate (2013–2015); author of four collections of poetry, including *Eldest Daughter* and *Kitchen Heat* (both LSU Press). Her poems have been used as text for classical and jazz composers.

Caroline Hill — artist and graduate of LSU; further art studies in Brooklyn, New York; she now paints in her hometown of New Orleans; recent show at Sullivan Art Gallery.

Jackson Hill — photojournalist; operated Southern Lights studio in New Orleans for many years; taught at NOCCA; jacksonhillphotography.com.

Roberta Whitman Hoff — originally from New England, now lives in New Orleans with her two cats. She's an English major and recently published a horror poem about abuse against women (Black Spot Books).

Barry Ivker — poet, teacher, lifetime lover of music and dancing; author of *Sonata in F# minor, Haggedah, Promised Land,* and *Out of the Depths* (plays).

Julia Johnson — native New Orleanian poet; author of *Subsidence, Naming the Afternoon,* and *The Falling Horse*. She has served as editor of *Mississippi Review* and for *The Collected Poems of Jane Gentry;* she's a founding director of the new MFA program in Creative Writing at the University of Kentucky.

T.R. Johnson — has hosted a jazz radio program at WWOZ and taught at Tulane University for several years. He's the author of *New Orleans A Writer's City* (Cambridge, 2023). He kayaks in the swamps a bit and maintains a mini jungle behind his Bywater house.

Mason Joiner — originally from North Louisiana; most recently he has been teaching at Delgado Community College in New Orleans.

Julie Kane — Louisiana Poet Laureate (2011–2013); native of Boston, Massachusetts; professor of creative writing at Northwestern State University in Natchitoches. She is author of *Naked Ladies* (LSU Press, 2025), *Jazz Funeral, Body and Soul* and *Mothers of Ireland*.

Robin Kemp — Louisiana native, journalist, professor and poet; currently reports from Savannah, Georgia; earned an MFA in creative writing at the University of New Orleans.

Bill Lavender — poet, novelist, musician, and construction worker living in New Orleans. His latest books are *city of god* (MadHat 2026), *My ID* (Blaze-VOX), and *Three Letters* (novellas, Spuyten Duyvil). He is the publisher at Lavender Ink/Dialogos, and current director of New Orleans Poetry Festival.

Mark Marley — longtime public school educator; graduate of Jesuit High School; author of *The Great Reveal*; award-winning long-distance runner.

Charlotte Mears — former resident of Louisiana; MFA from the University of Arkansas; now residing in Mississippi; she's the author of *Sweet Air* and *Winds of NY*.

Sean F. Munro — writing instructor at Delgado Community College; lively open-mike poet; helps direct the New Orleans Poetry Festival and co-curates The Splice Poetry Series.

Geoff Munsterman — poet who grew up in Plaquemines Parish; graduate of New Orleans Center for the Creative Arts; now writes and manages a bookstore (Crescent Books, in downtown New Orleans); editor and book designer; author of *Because the Stars Shine Through It*.

James Nolan — native New Orleanian poet, translator and creative writing teacher; author of *Perpetual Care* (short stories), *Why I Live in the Forest, What Moves Is Not the Wind, Nasty Water* (poems), *Pablo Neruda, Stones of the Sky* (translation), and *Higher Ground* (novel).

Biljana D. Obradovic — professor of English at Xavier University with four collections of poems, including *Little Disruptions*. She's also served as a translator and editor for several books including Dubravka Djuric's *The Politics of Hope (After the War)*. Biljana's fifth collection of poems, *Called by Distances*, was published by LSU Press in 2026.

Niyi Osundare — one of the most honored poets of Africa, he has taught creative writing at the University of New Orleans and University of Ibadan in Nigeria; and performed in many countries. Osundare's many awards include The NOMA Award (Africa's most prestigious book award). Among his many publications: *Green: sighs of our ailing planet* (Black Widow Press).

Sue Owen — taught creative writing at LSU; author of *Hurricane in a Bad Mood, The Book of Winter*, and *Nursery Rhymes for the Dead*.

Melinda Palacio — bi-lingual poet who resides in Louisiana and California; author of *Folsom Lockdown, How Fire Is a Story, Waiting* (poems), and *Ocotillo Dreams* (novel).

Alison Pelegrin — Louisiana Poet Laureate (2023–2025); author of *Our Lady of Bewilderment* and *Waterlines* (both with LSU Press); started and continues work with prisoners in the Lifelines Poetry Project. She also serves as Writer-in-Residence at Southeastern Louisiana University.

Valentine Pierce — creative artist; born and raised in New Orleans; U.S. Army veteran; author of *Geometry of the Heart* and *Up Decatur*.

Emma Pierson — vocalist, teacher/speech pathologist; has performed in over 50 ballets and operatic ballets; she is author of *New Orleans: City of My Heart* (poems).

Paul Pines — poet and psychotherapist, he published nine books of poetry; although from New York, he spent much time in New Orleans; his collections include: *New Orleans Variations (poems)* and *The Tin Angel* (a novel.)

Brad Richard — poet and instructor of creative writing at New Orleans Center for the Creative Arts and The Willow School; author of *Habitations, Parasite Kingdom*, and, most recently, *Turned Earth* (LSU Press).

James M. Robinson — taught Spanish for several years in Huntsville, Alabama; often visits family in Louisiana; author of *The Caterpillars at Saint Bernard* and *Boca Del Rio in the Afternoon.*

Ed Ruzicka — has directed the Louisiana Poetry Society organization; he hails from Baton Rouge; worked as an occupational therapist; he's the author of *Squalls, My Life in Cars, Engines of Belief*, and *In the Wind.*

Bessie Senette — grew up along the bayous of Lafourche and Terrebonne parishes; she now lives in Lafayette; author of *Cutting the Clouds, A Bayou Mystic's Poems, Musings and Imaginings*, and the forthcoming *Louisiana Pines, Homeland Poems and Vignettes.*

Martha Serpas — native of South Louisiana; author of *Double Effect, The Diener*, and *The Dirty Side of the Storm*. She co-produced *Veins in the Gulf*, a documentary on Louisiana's coastal land loss. She teaches creative writing at the University of Houston and is a hospital chaplain.

H.R. "Stoney" Stoneback — poet, folksinger, scholar; sang in the French Quarter during the 1960s; earned a PhD at Vanderbilt; taught at the State University of New York at New Paltz; author of *Singing the Springs, Hurricane Hymn,* and other collections.

Clint Smith — graduate of Ben Franklin High School in New Orleans; poet and journalist; author of *Counting Descent, Above Ground*, and *How the Word Was Passed*. His essays have appeared in *The Atlantic, The New Yorker, The New York Times Magazine*, and *The Paris Review.*

John Warner Smith — Louisiana Poet Laureate (2019–2021); author of *Our Shut Eyes: New & Selected Poems on Race in America* (MadHat Press), *Muhammad's Mountain* (Lavender Ink), *Spirits of the Gods* (ULL Press), and *For All Those Men* (novel). He resides in the Lafayette area.

John P. Travis — compiler of *Diving Into Nature*; publisher of Portals Press; former journalist; teacher; and author of *Pitching in the Dark* (novel) and *J.J'.s Journal (*short stories*).*

Michael S. True — poet, visual artist and singer/songwriter; U.S. Navy veteran; long-time performer at The Neutral Ground and The Maple Leaf; author of *Diabolical Seas, On Shaky Ground* (poems), and *Miracles and Wonders* (short stories).

Gordon Walmsley — native New Orleanian who has established his writing and editing career in Copenhagen, Denmark; graduate of Tulane Law; author of *Dreams of a Lifetime, Echoes of a River*, and *Touchstones.*

Jonathan E. Warren — poet, carpenter and a player of Native American flutes; hails from St. Charles Parish but often plays in bands in Orleans and Jefferson parishes; author of *Go to the River* and *Who Is The Drummer.*

Andy Young — grew up in West Virginia; she has taught creative writing at the New Orleans Center for the Creative Arts and lived in Egypt during recent revolutionary times. She's author of *Museum of the Soon Departed* (2025) and *All Night It Is Morning*; her work has been translated into several languages.